I See Rectangles

By Czeena Devera

 This rectangle has shoes.

This rectangle has toys.

 4

This rectangle has flowers.

This rectangle has dots.

 This rectangle has lunch.

This rectangle has letters.

 This rectangle has movies.

This rectangle has family.

This rectangle has sprinkles.

This rectangle has stories.

This rectangle has music.

This rectangle has mail.

Word List

rectangle   lunch   stories

shoes   letters   music

toys   movies   mail

flowers   family

dots   sprinkles

48 Words

This rectangle has shoes.
This rectangle has toys.
This rectangle has flowers.
This rectangle has dots.
This rectangle has lunch.
This rectangle has letters.
This rectangle has movies.
This rectangle has family.
This rectangle has sprinkles.
This rectangle has stories.
This rectangle has music.
This rectangle has mail.

CHERRY BLOSSOM PRESS

Published in the United States of America by Cherry Lake Publishing Group
Ann Arbor, Michigan
www.cherrylakepublishing.com

Photo Credits: © megerka_megerka/Shutterstock.com, front cover, 1; © Halfpoint/Shutterstock.com, 2; © Makistock/Shutterstock.com, 3; © antpkr/Shutterstock.com, 4; © azazello photo studio/Shutterstock.com, 5; © Africa Studio/Shutterstock.com, 6; © Monkey Business Images/Shutterstock.com, 7; © Tero Vesalainen/Shutterstock.com, 8; © Aleksandra Suzi/Shutterstock.com, 9; © Lifestyle Travel Photo/Shutterstock.com, 10, 14; © Rawpixel.com/Shutterstock.com, 11; © Seeme/Shutterstock.com, 12; © NDanko/Shutterstock.com, 13; © Duntrune Studios/Shutterstock.com, back cover

Cherry Blossom Press is an imprint of Cherry Lake Publishing Group.

Library of Congress Cataloging-in-Publication Data

Names: Devera, Czeena, author.
Title: I see rectangles / Czeena Devera.
Description: Ann Arbor, Michigan : Cherry Lake Publishing, 2021. | Series: Shapes | Audience: Grades K-1 | Summary: "Spot rectangle shapes in everyday objects in this book. Beginning readers will gain confidence with the Whole Language approach to literacy, a combination of sight words and repetition. Bold, colorful photographs correlate directly to the text to help guide readers as they engage with the book"— Provided by publisher.
Identifiers: LCCN 2020030266 (print) | LCCN 2020030267 (ebook) | ISBN 9781534179868 (paperback) | ISBN 9781534180871 (pdf) | ISBN 9781534182585 (ebook)
Subjects: LCSH: Rectangles—Juvenile literature.
Classification: LCC QA482 .D483 2021 (print) | LCC QA482 (ebook) | DDC 516/.154—dc23
LC record available at https://lccn.loc.gov/2020030266
LC ebook record available at https://lccn.loc.gov/2020030267

Cherry Lake Publishing Group would like to acknowledge the work of the Partnership for 21st Century Learning, a Network of Battelle for Kids. Please visit *http://www.battelleforkids.org/networks/p21* for more information.

Printed in the United States of America
Corporate Graphics